1945 ~ 1976
America Today

Written by NAUNERLE FARR

Edited by D'ANN CALHOUN

Illustrated by NARDO CRUZ

Editorial consultant LAWRENCE W. BLOCH

A VINCENT FAGO PRODUCTION

Pendulum Press, Inc.
West Haven, Connecticut

ISBN 0-88301-234-0

Published by
PENDULUM PRESS, INC.
An Academic Industries, Inc., Company
The Academic Building
Saw Mill Road
West Haven, Connecticut 06516

Printed in the United States of America

To the Teacher:

With educators everywhere concerned about the literacy of the nation's children, attention has been focused primarily on the reading curriculum. Reading teachers can select from literally thousands of varied programs for their classes. Yet social studies teachers, faced with an equal amount of material to cover, are often at a loss. Although many history texts are available, they all seem to offer information alone at the expense of motivation. Out of this understanding the **Basic Illustrated History of America** series was developed.

Motivation is the basic premise and the outstanding strength of these texts. Each book was written in the belief that children will learn and remember whatever they find enjoyable. Through illustration, they are drawn into the reading matter, and learning begins.

Besides motivating, the illustrations provide clues to the meanings of words. Unfamiliar vocabulary is defined in footnotes. Every volume in the series has been edited to simplify the reading. And, since the interest level extends as far as the adult reader, students in all grades—even in remedial classes—will enjoy these texts. Finally, companion student activity books guide the reading with vocabulary drills and exercises on comprehension.

The **Basic Illustrated History of America** series, then, offers a new concept in the teaching of American history, yet one which does not subordinate content to form. Meticulously researched historical data provides the authenticity for costumes and architecture in each era. Together, the features of this unique series will make learning an enjoyable experience for the student— and a rewarding one for the teacher.

                                                                    The editors

contents

Efforts toward integration in the South move along quickly during the administrations of Truman and Eisenhower 6-18

Both America and the Soviet Union send men into space; Castro takes over the Cuban government 19-22

John F. Kennedy becomes the thirty-fifth president of the United States; he sets up the Peace Corps and begins his work on civil rights 23-29

Kennedy keeps Russian missiles out of Cuba; in November, 1963, he is assassinated; Lyndon B. Johnson is sworn in as the next president 30-36

Both negroes and chicanos continue to fight for their rights; Martin Luther King, Jr. and Robert Kennedy are assassinated 37-46

During Nixon's term as president, a man walks on the moon; Nixon himself visits China. . .47-53

The Watergate hearings cause Nixon to resign; Gerald Ford becomes president on the eve of America's 200th birthday 54-59

Questions for study. 60-61

The thirteenth amendment to the Constitution made slavery against the law anywhere in the United States. When it passed in the House of Representatives in 1865, there was wild cheering and great happiness.

For the slaves themselves, a new way of life began.

At a meeting of the American Anti-Slavery Society in New York, William Lloyd Garrison wanted to break up the group.

We don't need an anti-slavery group after slavery is killed.

But Wendell Phillips disagreed.

I fear you are too hopeful. We still have a long way to go!

Negroes are still fighting for their rights. Many of these have been won since World War II.

In the 1936 Olympic games at Berlin, Jesse Owens, a black American, broke several world records.

Ralph Metcalf and Eddie Tolan also set records.

Adolf Hitler, a man who hated negroes, was very angry. He left the stands rather than watch Owens and other black Americans receive their medals.

In World War II, more than a million black Americans fought in our armed forces against Hitler and the Nazis. Types of service and training were opened to them that had been closed to them before.

Integration* in the army began in 1945 when black soldiers fought beside white soldiers in Germany.

Eighteen liberty ships were named for negroes.

Captain Hugh Mulzac, report to the *S.S. Booker T. Washington.*

In the merchant marine, 24,000 blacks served in mixed crews. Some were commanded by black officers.

Under Colonel Benjamin O. Davis, Jr. the 332nd fighter group, all black, flew more than 3,000 missions in Europe.

*placing blacks and whites together in daily life

They destroyed 300 enemy planes. Eighty-eight pilots, including Colonel Davis, received the Distinguished Flying Cross.*

In 1950 in the Korean War, black and white soldiers fought together in integrated units. Davis served as chief of staff of United States forces.

In 1946, Truman set up the President's Committee on Civil Rights.

Helping people keep their freedom is the duty of every government state, federal,** and local.

But when state or local governments fail...the federal government must step in.

*a special medal for great bravery in air battles
**national

By his order Truman ended segregation* in the armed forces and in federal jobs. But he could not push stronger civil rights laws through Congress. He was defeated by southern Democrats and Republicans.

The next civil rights act came from the Supreme Court on May 17, 1954.

In public education, "separate but equal" has no place. When black and white schools are separate, they are not equal.

George Hayes, Thurgood Marshall, and James Nabrit, black lawyers who led the fight, were very happy.

But Governor Byrnes of South Carolina was not glad at all.

I am shocked! All our people, white and colored, must use their common sense.

In 1956, President Eisenhower made a speech at the Miami airport.

People must be truly equal in their hearts. Then they will be equal under the law.

*keeping blacks and whites separate in daily life

Between 1954 and 1956, several hundred schools throughout the country integrated their classes.

On September 3, 1957, a desegregation plan was to begin in Little Rock, Arkansas.

But the night before, Governor Faubus made a surprise television speech.

The NAACP doesn't like this plan. It admits only a few negro children to one senior high school.

It's not enough, of course, but at least it's a beginning.

We will not be able to keep order if integration is carried out tomorrow.

I am therefore placing National Guardsmen outside Central High to act only as soldiers.

A message came from the school board.

They tell us not to send negro children to Central High tomorrow. They will ask the federal judge for orders.

The next morning the federal judge gave an order.

I will take the governor's word that the soldiers are neutral.* I order the desegregation plan to begin now!

On September 4, nine negro children tried to go to Central High. The National Guard was there. So was a mob.

They're coming! Here they come!

Fifteen-year-old Elizabeth Ann Eckford walked quietly up to a school door.

A soldier barred her way.

Go on home!

*not on either side in an argument

Alone, Elizabeth Ann walked back past the crowd to the bus stop.

What are you doing, you nigger lover?

She's scared. She's just a little girl!

A white woman went over to comfort her.

By the next day, the FBI had agents at Little Rock. Governor Faubus spoke again.

I have wired the president to stop sending FBI agents here!

That's telling 'em, Governor!

Mr. Eisenhower made his reply.

All I can tell Governor Faubus is that I will follow the Constitution at all times!

The trouble continued. Finally Eisenhower ordered a thousand soldiers to Little Rock. He ordered 10,000 members of the Arkansas National Guard to put down the mob. For the first time since Reconstruction, soldiers were sent into the South to protect the negroes.

On September 25, the nine black children joined the 2,000 white children at Central High.

There was trouble in the city as well as at the school. Homes of integration leaders were bombed.

Crosses were burned on their lawns.

Segregation leaders kept trouble alive in Little Rock for three years. But at last Ernest Green became the first black graduate of an integrated Central High School.

By 1962 the high schools in Little Rock were integrated. The battle was not won, but at least it was well begun.

★★★★★★★★★★★★★★

On an evening in 1955, Mrs. Rosa Parks got on a bus, tired from work.

It was in Montgomery, Alabama, that Jefferson Davis had become president of the Confederacy. Southern feelings had always run high here.

★★★★★★★★★★★★★★★★★★★★★★★★★★★★★★★★

★★★★★★★★★★★★★

The Montgomery bus boycott* was under way. Since sixty-five percent of the riders had been negroes, the buses were nearly empty.

Sure I'm tired, walking four miles home after working all day. But I won't take a bus!

There were many evening meetings. Again and again, the blacks listened to Martin Luther King, Jr.

Our victory will not be for Montgomery's negroes alone. It will be a victory for justice...a victory for democracy!

This is not a war between the white and the negro...this is bigger. If we are arrested every day, we must not hate. We must use the weapon of love.

In November, 1956, the Supreme Court spoke.

This court agrees that bus segregation is against the Constitution.

this happens when a group of people decide to have nothing to do with a certain product or service.

Shortly before Christmas, the boycott ended.

You mean we just get on the bus? We can take the first seat we come to?

That's the law, now! No "colored" parts of the bus!

Inside, blacks and whites sat together.

Yes, sir, that's right.

I see this isn't going to be a "White Christmas."

I can't understand what all the fuss has been about!

A reporter talked to a black grandmother.

Jim Crow,* he's more than a hundred years old, and real tired. We've put up long enough with tired things.

* a symbol of the negro as a slave; this name had been used since Civil War times

Shortly after the soldiers were sent to Little Rock in 1957, there was news of a different kind.

The Soviet Union announced that it has sent a man-made earth satellite* into space yesterday.

They're making history!

Can we see it?

Satellite tracking became a popular thing to do.

Look! There it is!

Imagine—500 miles up!

And going 18,000 miles an hour! It's hard to believe!

In 1958, Congress set up the National Aeronautics and Space Administration.

The United States believes that activities in space should be devoted to peaceful purposes.

But it was more than that.

We've been building long-range bombers. But if the Soviet Union can build such powerful rockets, she can build missiles** to reach the United States.

We'd best get on with our missile program!

The race to put a man on the moon was on!

*an object put into space to travel around a planet
**bombs that can be fired by a rocket

On April 12, 1961, there was another announcement from Moscow radio.

Russia has sent a man into space. His name is Yuri Gagarin.

I can hardly believe it!

On May 6, the Americans had their turn to be happy. They could even watch it on television.

Two...one...zero...blast off!

They listened to Alan Shepard's words during his trip.

All systems go! Everything A-O.K. Coming in for a landing!

It's the greatest thing that ever happened!

They could see for themselves, as Shepard stepped onto the ship, that he was all right.

Things were also taking place on the other side of the world. For seven years, French soldiers in Indo-China had been fighting a communist group, the Vietminh. Under President Eisenhower, the United States had been trying to prevent the spread of communism. We aided the French with money, bombers, supplies, and air force workers to service the planes.

On May 7, 1954, after fifty-five days, the French base of Dienbienphu fell to the communists.

In Geneva, on July 21, the French and the Vietminh signed a treaty.

In September U.S. Secretary of State Dulles announced a new treaty.

The United States, Great Britain, France, Australia, New Zealand, the Philippine Republic, Thailand, and Pakistan have formed the Southeast Asia Treaty Organization (SEATO). They would try to keep the communists from taking other countries in the area.

The governments of Laos and Cambodia were recognized by the communists. Vietnam was divided into two parts. The north part of the country became communist.

In Cuba, in 1959, soldiers under Fidel Castro fought and won over President Batista.

The United States quickly recognized the Castro government.

| Batista was a dictator.* The Cuban people had a hard time. | Castro promised to build a democracy. He promised to hold free elections. |

But Castro put off the elections. He had hundreds of his enemies killed. And he began to turn more and more to the Soviet Union.

Thousands of people escaped from Cuba to Florida.

*a ruler who gives his people only the rights he wants them to have

In 1960, Americans held an election for president. The two candidates,* Senator John F. Kennedy and Vice-president Richard M. Nixon, met in several television talks.

No Roman Catholic had ever been elected president. Kennedy, a Catholic, spoke to the Houston Ministerial Association on September 12.

I believe in an America where Church and State are truly separate.

In a close election, Kennedy, a great-grandson of Irish immigrants, became the first Catholic and the youngest man ever elected president.

Soon after, Kennedy announced the start of a Peace Corps. It would send Americans to help people in other countries.

It will not be easy. None...will be paid. They will live at the same level as the people of the country....

*people who hope to be elected to an office

World boy scouts, huh?

It's silly! Americans want to make money, not do good.

But American youth did want to help. By September of 1963, 10,000 were serving in the Peace Corps.

With skills in teaching, farming, or health work, more than 12,000 people served in fifty-three nations. In Tanganyika Jeremiah Parson taught road-building.

In Nepal Barbara Wylie taught English.

American youth answered President Kennedy's call for service.

Kennedy asked Congress to step up unemployment insurance,* mainly in areas like Appalachia where jobs were scarce. He also asked Congress for aid to workers, to schools, to farmers, and to people over sixty-five.

Even before he was elected, he said that he would work to make blacks and whites really equal.

Only a president willing to use all the help he can get will be able to solve the problems of different races in our country.

Much of this work was given to the Attorney General, the president's brother, Robert Kennedy.

People will not like it if you make me the Attorney General! They will say it's just because I'm your brother.

Should I lose the best man for the job, just because he is my brother?

Robert Kennedy brought into the Justice Department a strong staff, including Burke Marshall.

I want you as my helper in the Civil Rights division.

There is a lot to be done.

*money to pay for food and rent for those who don't have jobs

In 1961, black students began a number of Freedom Rides against segregation in bus, rail, and air travel.

Busloads of people, both black and white, rode into the South. Entering Alabama, one bus was stoned and burned.

It's not just riding in the back of the bus! It's the separate waiting rooms, separate ticket windows, and separate toilets. And all of them are dirty!

And too bad if we get hungry! The lunch counter won't serve us.

Let's just go and sit in the white areas! We won't be noisy, we'll just sit!

The Attorney General sent 500 soldiers to Alabama to keep order. The governor of Alabama was angry.

At bus stations, the riders were met by angry mobs.

Tell him that we did not need their help and we do not want their help! We do not want them here in Alabama!

Kennedy answered.

Tell the governor that the United States government needs to know that its people will be safe in Alabama.

As a result of the Freedom Riders, Kennedy got an order from the Interstate Commerce Commission. It would not allow segregation in trains, buses, and stations.

In January, 1961, James Meredith, a young black air force man from Mississippi, tried to get into the University of Mississippi at Oxford.

Governor Ross Barnett said that he would not obey the law.

Mississippians were angry.

There's never been a negro at Ole Miss. We'll see to it there never will be!

Helped by the NAACP, Meredith went to court on the grounds that he had been turned down because of his race. After a long battle, the court ruled in Meredith's favor.

We will not give in to the evil forces around us.

On September 20, 1962, Meredith went with a group of soldiers to register. Barnett barred his way and read him a long speech.

Here is the answer! Take it and live by it!

For days the trouble went on. But the two sides stood firm.

The Mississippi courts are as high as any other court. I am going to obey the laws of Mississippi!

My job is to see that the laws of the United States are kept. I intend to do my job.

At last President Kennedy called out the Mississippi National Guard. He moved army troops to a base near Mississippi.

President Kennedy spoke to the country.

If this country should ever reach the point where any group would not obey our Constitution, then no law would stand, and no citizen would be safe.

In the late afternoon, Meredith arrived at the university with a group of soldiers who brought him to his own building.

Governor Barnett had given his word that the State Highway Patrol would keep order. But at sunset a crowd began to gather.

The state troopers left. Cars full of white men drove to the university.

For two hours the soldiers stood quietly. Some were bleeding from the bricks and bottles that were thrown. Then the crowd began to move in. Tear gas was fired.

More soldiers were called in. For fifteen hours a riot raged. Snipers* fired from the darkness. Two men were killed and hundreds were wounded. Cars and army trucks were burned.

Soon 5,000 soldiers guarded the university.

But Meredith attended classes, even though a small army was needed for the victory.

It was a long, lonely time until his graduation in 1963. But the step had been taken.

Three weeks later, the president again spoke to the American people. He told them the Soviet Union was building missile bases in Cuba.

The purpose of these bases must be to fire missiles at North and South America.

For two months there had been reports of Russian ships landing people, planes, and missiles in Cuba.

*people who shoot at others from a hiding place a long distance away.

Kennedy had ordered U-2 plane flights over Cuba to photograph the missile sights.

Back at the base, men studied the blown-up photographs.

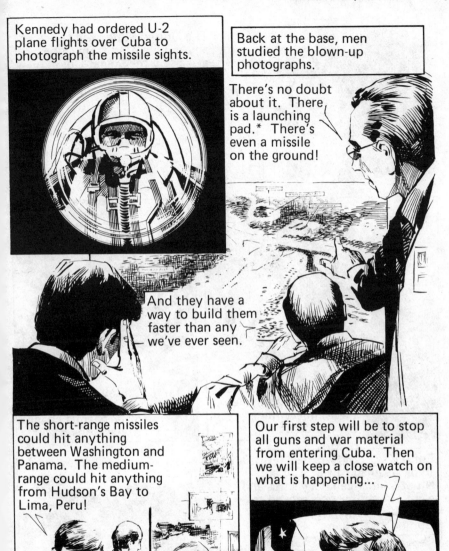

There's no doubt about it. There is a launching pad.* There's even a missile on the ground!

And they have a way to build them faster than any we've ever seen.

The short-range missiles could hit anything between Washington and Panama. The medium-range could hit anything from Hudson's Bay to Lima, Peru!

Our first step will be to stop all guns and war material from entering Cuba. Then we will keep a close watch on what is happening...

*the place from which rockets and missiles are fired.

The United States will consider any missile fired from Cuba as an attack by the Soviet Union on America. We must answer such an attack by firing missiles of our own.

What does it mean?

It means the Russians are setting up missile bases ninety miles off our coast!

Does it mean war?

If the Russians really want war, I'd say yes. If not, Kennedy has given them a chance to back down.

For days people worried. Russian ships steamed toward Cuba. Ninety American navy ships and eight aircraft carriers moved to keep the Russian ships from landing.

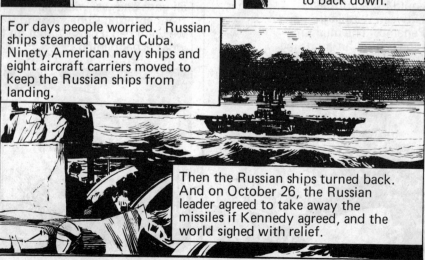

Then the Russian ships turned back. And on October 26, the Russian leader agreed to take away the missiles if Kennedy agreed, and the world sighed with relief.

On June 19, 1963, Kennedy sent to Congress an important bill on civil rights. On August 28, 200,000 people, mostly black but many white, gathered peacefully in Washington to show their support.

In the afternoon, Dr. Martin Luther King talked to the people.

I have a dream...that one day this nation will live out the true meaning of its creed: ...all men are created equal...

...that one day even the state of Mississippi...will be a place of freedom.

On November 22, 1963, President and Mrs. Kennedy flew to Dallas, Texas. There they were greeted by the Texas governor.

They drove through cheering crowds toward downtown Dallas.

Suddenly a sniper from a nearby building fired three shots. The president was wounded. The governor was injured. The whole world was shocked. A short time later, Lee Harvey Oswald, who had once lived in the Soviet Union, was arrested for the crime.

Ninety minutes after the president's death, the vice-president, Lyndon B. Johnson, was sworn in as the thirty-sixth president. He spoke the oath of office in the cabin of the president's plane as Mrs. Kennedy stood by.

Two days later, in sight of television viewers across the nation, Oswald was shot and killed in the Dallas jail by Jack Ruby.

Later, a special Presidential Commission of Investigation decided that Oswald had been acting alone.

Meanwhile, Johnson was trying to pick up the pieces.

This is a sad time for all people. We have suffered a great loss. But I will do my best. I ask your help—and God's.

People listened—and thought that the new president, LBJ, might do the job.

He's from Texas. He's the first southern president since the Civil War!

More than that, he's one of the best men ever to become president. I think he'll do a fine job.

On June 19, 1964, Congress passed the strong civil rights bill that both Johnson and Kennedy had worked for.

It will be our work to take the words of the law and make them the rules we follow.

We must fight against poor education, poor housing, and our past mistakes. It is our job to make things right again.

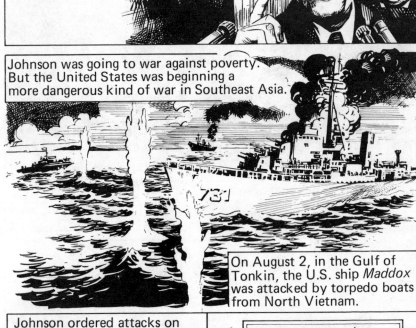

Johnson was going to war against poverty. But the United States was beginning a more dangerous kind of war in Southeast Asia.

On August 2, in the Gulf of Tonkin, the U.S. ship *Maddox* was attacked by torpedo boats from North Vietnam.

Johnson ordered attacks on shore bases in North Vietnam.

The Senate agreed.

Today the Senate agreed that the president should fight to defend the free states in Southeast Asia.

So did the American people. In November, Johnson was elected president in his own right.

With Johnson's victory, the Democrats won many seats in Congress. This helped the president to begin building his "Great Society". Congress passed the Economic Opportunity Act to train young people for jobs. They also passed bills for aid to education, Medicare,* and civil rights.

A new cabinet post was made: the Department of Housing and Urban Development. Johnson chose Robert Weaver as secretary.

The cities are in trouble sir. Could you tell me some of your plans?

In a poor negro area of Los Angeles called Watts, riots broke out in the hot August of 1965.

*a program for paying the medical bills of people over 65

Fighting, stealing, and burning spread over a thirteen square mile area. It went on for four days. Twenty-one were killed, 600 hurt. 20,000 National Guard soldiers were needed to calm things down.

Martin Luther King, Jr. talked about love. Other blacks, in their anger, turned to "black power" and hate.

In 1967, in Cleveland, Ohio, Carl Stokes was elected mayor. He was the first negro mayor of a large U.S. city.

In July, 1967, a riot broke out in Detroit. More than forty people were killed; blocks of buildings were burned; thousands were left homeless.

President Johnson spoke on television.

We must attack the things which lead to sorrow and anger.

Close to Watts in Los Angeles is another poor area, a "barrio", where the Mexican-American people were beginning to speak out.

There are five million Mexican-Americans in the United States. We are poorer; our housing is worse; our level of education is lower than any other group! What about us?

In California we out-number the blacks by two to one. But where are the programs to help *us*?

Man, if east L.A. ever blows, it will really blow!

In March, 1968, the students of five high schools in Los Angeles walked out. They were all Mexican-Americans.

VIVA LA RAZA

VIVA LA RAZA!

VIVA LA Revolucion

The U.S. government began to help. The committee on Mexican-American affairs was set up to help solve the problems of these poor people. Vicente T. Ximenes was chosen to head the group.

The largest Mexican-American problem was that of the farm workers. They earned only $1,500 a year. Their homes were very poor. So Cesar Chavez began the United Farm Workers of America, a group which became well-known during the grape workers' strike in 1965.

The most important event was the twenty-five day march of the workers from Delano to Sacramento.

Starting with seventy-five men, the marchers grew to a crowd of 4,000. They arrived at the state capital on Easter Sunday.

Martin Luther King, Jr. sent his good wishes to Chavez.

The fight must be fought on many fronts—in the slums, in the factories, and in the fields. Our separate fights are really one...

Following Truman and Eisenhower, President Kennedy had promised to keep the communists out of South Vietnam. It was a special kind of fighting.

A new type of soldier was trained to fight it. They were a special group of guerrilla fighters,* the Green Berets.

This is a new kind of war... fought not in large battles, but in secret attacks...

Truman had sent thirty-five men to help. Eisenhower had sent 500 more. Still the communists were winning. So Kennedy sent 15,000 soldiers.

President Johnson sent even more men. By 1966, 375,000 Americans were fighting in Vietnam.

Your main job is to train the South Vietnamese soldiers. But if you have to do some fighting yourself, you may do it.

*soldiers who fight by making small surprise attacks which soon wear out their enemies

Many Americans were upset by this all-out war. Some young men burned their draft cards.

In October, 1967, 35,000 people marched on Washington. They placed flowers in the guns of the police.

Senator Eugene McCarthy of Minnesota announced that he would run against Johnson in the Democratic presidential primaries.* He would stand for those who were against the war.

Soon Robert F. Kennedy, brother of the late president, made the same announcement.

*the elections in which each party chooses the man who will run for president.

Then two events sent waves of sorrow, shock, and anger over the country.

APRIL 5

Dr. Martin Luther King, Jr., who preached love and brotherhood, was shot in Memphis last night by a sniper...

Oh, my God -- no!

The president, speaking from the White House, has set Sunday as a day of mourning for Dr. King.

From all over the country, black and white leaders gathered to attend Dr. King's funeral.

Two months later, on June 6, 1968, Robert Kennedy celebrated winning the California Democratic election primary.

Then shots rang out. Now it was Robert Kennedy, friend of the blacks, the chicanos,* of all young Americans, who had been shot.

Robert Kennedy died on June 6, 1968. Dr. King's killer, James Earl Ray, was later captured, tried, and sentenced to ninety-nine years in prison. Sirhan Sirhan, the killer of Robert Kennedy, received the same sentence.

Once again thousands gathered to mourn -- and to wonder what was happening to America.

*Mexican-Americans.

The war protests grew. By 1968, about 10,000 young Americans had left for Canada to escape the draft.

President Johnson made Thurgood Marshall the first negro justice on the Supreme Court.

And Shirley Chisholm, a Democrat from New York, became the first negro congresswoman.

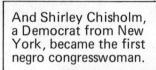

My rise has been swift. I know I am a symbol.

On March 31, President Johnson spoke to Americans on television.

I am taking the first step to stop the war. I have ordered our planes... to make no attacks except north of the demilitarized zone.*

*an area which neither army controls.

There is unrest in America now. I will not accept another term as your president.

I can't believe it! Johnson won't run again!

In 1964, he had the greatest vote in history... and now this.

That's what the Vietnam war has done.

On August 8, 1968, at Miami Beach, the Republican party chose Richard M. Nixon as its candidate.

In Chicago on August 28, Hubert Humphrey was chosen as the Democratic candidate.

This time there's a difference— this time we're going to win!

I say to America... turn away from anger and hatred!

In November, in a close election, Richard Nixon became president.

In his inauguration address, Nixon spoke of peace.

My job will be to bring the American people together!

The greatest honor history can give is the title of peacemaker...

Both the American and the Russian space programs had been continuing. On July 16, 1969, the American Apollo II blasted off for the moon.

102 hours and forty-six minutes later, Neil Armstrong radioed back to earth.

Tranquillity Base here. The Eagle has landed.

Then, as a world-wide audience of 600,000,000 people watched, men walked on another world. In New York, thousands watched the moonwalk on large screens set up in Central Park.

That's one small step for man, one giant leap for mankind.

Planting an American flag on the moon, Neil Armstrong saluted it.

And from the White House, President Nixon congratulated the astronauts.

This certainly has to be the most historic telephone call ever made!

On October 15, 1969, all over America people gathered in a rally for peace.

But there were other protests...

and workers' marches.

In the spring of 1970, America seemed to be blowing apart. There were bombings, bomb threats, fires, student revolts, and the take-over of college buildings. Then came the Kent State University shootings.

At Kent State in Ohio, National Guard soldiers fired into a crowd of rioting students. Four of the students were killed.

All over the country students went on strike. Four hundred colleges were closed.

Many students spent their time getting people to sign anti-war papers.

By April 15, Nixon had taken 115,000 soldiers out of Vietnam. Several plans to aid the poor and the nation's cities were before Congress. Plans to help save our land, air, and water were already working. And Henry Kissinger, the president's chief adviser on foreign affairs, made a secret visit to the People's Republic of China.

In July, newsmen reported the reason for Kissinger's visit.

It has been announced that a meeting will take place between President Nixon and Chinese Premier Chou En-lai.

The President and Mrs. Nixon will visit the Republic of China early next year.

Nixon visiting the head of Communist China! That really is news!

For nearly twenty-five years the United States had helped the Nationalist Chinese government of Chiang Kai-shek. We had voted against admitting to the United Nations the communist Republic of China.

But on October 25, 1971, the United States was defeated, and the U.N. would admit the Chinese communists.

The Chinese Nationalists were sent away, and their delegates left the assembly.

On the morning of February 21, 1972, Air Force One touched down on a runway in China. It brought President Nixon for the first visit of an American president behind the Bamboo Curtain of Communist China.

The American people watched on television as Nixon left the plane.

To Premier Chou En-lai, Nixon held out the hand of friendship, and Chou En-lai took it.

Later that day, Nixon was received by Chairman Mao Tse-tung.

Americans traveled around China by way of television as the cameras followed Nixon.

They visited the Great Wall of China and its watchtowers, dating from 1368 A.D.

Nixon and Premier Chou announced together the need for American and Chinese talks. The United States agreed that the island of Taiwan belonged to China. This ended American support of nationalist China,* and paved the way for better feelings with Chou's government.

*independent or non-communist China.

In May, 1972, Nixon visited the Soviet Union. He and party leader Brezhnev signed two papers putting limits on the growth of nuclear weapons* supplies.

We want to be remembered...by the fact that we made the world a more peaceful one for all peoples...

This is a great victory for all peaceloving people. Peace is our common goal.

But other things were happening in Washington. At 2 A.M. on June 17, the police answered a call from the Watergate building. They arrested several men who had broken into the offices of the Democratic National Headquarters.

Don't shoot— we give up!

One of the men arrested was James McCord. He was a member of the Republican Committee to Re-elect the President. In the notebook of one man was the name of a White House worker.

*atomic-powered weapons

In November President Nixon was re-elected. On January 23, 1973, he appeared on television with an announcement.

From Defense Secretary Laird on June 27 there was more news.

...Today we have made an agreement to end the war and bring peace..in Vietnam and Southeast Asia.

From now on the army will use only volunteers.* The draft has ended.

But the Watergate break-in and cover-up led to a Senate study of elections. The Senate was very interested in the workings of the 1972 campaign for president.

The Ervin committee opened its hearings in the Senate on May 17, 1973. The first witness was Robert Odle, manager of the re-election office staff.

Continuing through the summer, the hearings were followed on television by the nation.

*people who join a group because they want to, not because they are forced

On April 30, because of the Watergate cover-up, Nixon's two top aides resigned.* Nixon himself appeared on television to state that he had not known about it.

Tonight I ask for your prayers, to help me in everything I do. God bless America, and God bless each and every one of you.

On August 29, Judge John J. Sirica ordered that tape recordings of presidential talks be given to him.

...ordered that Richard M. Nixon ...is commanded to give up the tapes...

The president refused.

On October 11, vice-president Agnew appeared before Judge Walter E. Hoffman in Baltimore. He admitted that he had not paid his income tax in 1967.

He also resigned as vice-president.

On December 6, Gerald R. Ford was sworn in as vice-president of the United States.

*gave up their jobs.

On Saturday evening, July 27, 1974, the thirty-eight members of the House Judiciary Committee voted for the impeachment* of President Nixon.

On August 8, President Nixon appeared on television again before the American people.

The next day Nixon said goodbye to members of his cabinet and staff.

*putting a high-ranking official on trial for doing wrong

Then for the last time as president he boarded the plane that had taken him all over the world, and flew home to California.

Once more, on August 9, Justice Burger gave the oath of office to Gerald Ford, this time as President of the United States.

Then Gerald Ford spoke to the nation.

I believe that truth is the glue that holds government together. That bond, though strained, is unbroken...

As we bind up the wounds of Watergate, more painful than those of foreign wars, let us restore the Golden Rule to politics.

On September 9, President Ford sent a pardon to Nixon, explaining his reasons.

. . . many months and perhaps more years will have to pass before Richard Nixon could have a fair trial. During this long period, anger would once again rise in this country...

On January 21, 1977, a Democrat from Georgia was sworn in as the next president of the United States.

I, Jimmy Carter, do solemnly swear . . .

He's the first president from the Deep South since the Civil War!

His first remarks were addressed to Gerald Ford.

For myself and for our nation I want to thank my predecessor* for all he has done to heal our land . . .

I have no new dream to set forth today . . .

*a person who comes before someone else

His address ended, he surprised and delighted the crowd by walking the one and a half miles to the White House.

He is *walking!*

Wow! No bullet-proof limousine!*

In 1801, Thomas Jefferson had walked. In 1977, it was Jimmy Carter, a man of the people, walking towards his new responsibilities.

Many years ago, having finished his work at the Constitutional Convention, Benjamin Franklin was asked a question.

As we move forward in history we will continue to try... remembering, as President Kennedy said, that it will not be easy.

A republic, if you can keep it.

Mr. Franklin, what have you given us?

No one expects that our life will be easy...History will not permit it...But we are still the keystone in the arch of Freedom. And I think we will continue to do, as we have done in the past, our duty.

*a long, elegant automobile used for very special occasions

Words to know

boycott	launching pad
candidates	Medicare
chicanos	missiles
demilitarized zone	neutral
dictator	nuclear weapons
Distinguished Flying Cross	presidential primaries
federal	satellite
guerrilla fighters	segregation
impeachment	snipers
integration	unemployment insurance

Questions

1. During the 1960s, black Americans made many gains in their struggle for civil rights. What was gained in Little Rock, Arkansas between 1957 and 1962?

2. In the spring of 1961, both America and the Soviet Union did something for the first time. What was it?

3. What was the purpose of the Southeast Asia Treaty Organization (SEATO)?

4. What were the Freedom Riders trying to do?

5. Name some of the programs President Kennedy began during his term of office.

6. Under President Johnson, a new cabinet post was created. What was it? Who was its first secretary?

7. What other group besides blacks began to make themselves heard during the 1960s? Who spoke for them?

8. Early in 1968 two famous Americans were shot and killed. Who were they?

9. What great and historic event took place during the summer of 1969?

10. President Nixon resigned as president during the Watergate hearings. Why did he do this?

Match the following people with the things they are famous for:

1. Fidel Castro
2. Martin Luther King, Jr.
3. President John F. Kennedy
4. Thurgood Marshall
5. Neil Armstrong
6. Shirley Chisholm
7. Mao Tse-Tung
8. Mrs. Rosa Parks
9. Robert F. Kennedy
10. Chou En-Lai

a. chairman of the Chinese communist party

b. walked on the moon

c. first negro congresswoman

d. leader of Cuban government

e. negro woman who fought segregation on city buses

f. Chinese premier

g. first negro justice on the Supreme Court

h. President Kennedy's Attorney General

i. negro leader who taught peace and love

j. founder of the Peace Corps

Complete the following sentences

1. A special group set up in 1958 to explore the peaceful uses of rockets and space flight was the _____ .

2. _____ was the first black man to attend a southern university.

3. President Kennedy decided to stop all guns and war materials from entering Cuba in 1963 because _____.

4. _____ became the first negro mayor of a major U.S. city.

5. When the United States first became involved in the Vietnam war, we were simply trying to _____ .